SHOULD MY CHILD PLAY

AAU BASKETBALL?

5 TRUTHS EVERY PARENT MUST KNOW

SHOULD MY CHILD PLAY

AAU BASKET BALL?

5 TRUTHS EVERY PARENT MUST KNOW

ARLINGTON R. CALLIES

Should My Child Play AAU Basketball?:
5 Truths Every Parent Must Know

For information and permission requests, solicit the publisher at
the address below,
VC Publishing
PO Box 536
Argyle, TX 76226
info@VinsonCS.com

For interviews and booking information contact:
Arlington Callies
New Home Realty, LLC
arlington@newhomerealtytx.com
210-860-5381

ISBN: 979-8-9925783-7-9

Printed in the United States of America

First Edition

TABLE OF CONTENTS

PREFACE

This book was initially written in 2013. While some aspects of AAU basketball have changed, the core principles, challenges, and opportunities remain unchanged. This book aims to equip parents and young athletes with the knowledge necessary to make informed decisions about participating in AAU basketball. Whether you're new to the world of competitive youth sports or looking for guidance on navigating the AAU landscape, this book will help you understand the commitment, benefits, and potential pitfalls of the journey.

INTRODUCTION

If you examined the title of this book and decided to make a purchase, it's likely because your child is on an AAU (Amateur Athletic Union) team but receives little to no playing time. You may have invested a significant amount of time and money, and you might question whether it's worth chauffeuring your child and sometimes other kids to and from practice and games. The other parent's child plays twice as much as yours, but the two are friends, and you don't want to jeopardize that relationship.

Perhaps you feel frustrated because the coach starts a player and keeps them in the entire game. Although the player rarely attends practice, they are tall, fast, and talented.

In contrast, your child arrives at practice early, stays late, works diligently on their skills every day, maintains a positive attitude, and is very coachable, yet rarely gets to play. When your child finally has the chance to play in a game, they might take a bad shot, lose the ball, or fail to secure a rebound, causing the coach to pull them out. The coach may have a child on the team who isn't very good, but they play a lot because Dad is the coach. Alternatively, the coach's child could be an exceptional basketball player, yet a selfish one who always demands the ball— not a team player but someone who feels the offense is meant for them to score.

If you decided not to purchase the book, it could be because your child is a starter on the team and scores in bunches. They are in seventh or eighth grade and are already being considered by colleges nationwide. They are sure to be the next all-American at a division one college. They have skills and a great work ethic, are humble, coachable, and team players, do service work in the community, and bring home good grades.

You may be a single parent, and playing AAU basketball has taken your child off the streets and directed their attention on something worthwhile and enjoyable. It has given them an identity other than joining a gang or spending time with kids without direction. The coach is a great role model for your child and teaches Christian values and perseverance in facing adversity on and off the court.

Playing on the team instills accountability, loyalty, hard work, and respect for all humanity. As a parent, you are comfortable when they travel with the team to other cities and states to play basketball because your child is in a positive environment with strong role models. If they continue at their current pace, they will get a full-ride scholarship and a good education, and maybe—just maybe—a chance to play professional basketball.

I recommend buying this book anyway and giving it as a gift to someone who is struggling, regardless of whether you think their son or daughter should play AAU basketball.

The Amateur Athletic Union, or AAU, has existed for over 100 years and involves several sports, including track and field, basketball, and swimming. This book is focused on basketball, addressing most parents' questions and providing positive solutions to the most pressing concerns.

AAU is a venue that allows children to specialize and compete at a higher level in the sports they love. AAU, often referred to as select teams, includes some of the best players in the country. College coaches appreciate AAU because they can observe talented players compete in basketball over a single weekend tournament, cutting down on travel, food, and hotel expenses that they would typically incur when recruiting at various high schools across the country.

Many AAU teams travel across the state and country, participating in two to three tournaments each month. It is common for elementary and secondary school children to play year-round, honing their skills. Organizations like the San Antonio Rohawks and the Dallas Mustangs field several teams across various age groups, including children as young as six. Some teams are sponsored by major athletic apparel brands such as Adidas, Nike, and Reebok, and players wear their gear, including shoes, shirts, and bags. The tournament atmosphere is fantastic; sometimes, four to five games occur simultaneously.

So we are back to the million-dollar question: "Should I let my child play AAU basketball?" Should I allow my child to participate in any AAU sport?

Hopefully, the following chapters will answer your question.

DOES MY CHILD WANT TO PLAY AAU BASKETBALL?

The first question all parents should ask before putting a child on an AAU basketball team is whether the child truly wants to play the sport at that high level. It's essential that your child understands the commitment required and has the heart and passion for the game to compete at this level. It's not uncommon for a dad to want his child to play AAU basketball more than the child does, perhaps attempting to relive the game vicariously. Don't assume that your child wants to carry on the family legacy just because you were a great player or your uncle was an All-American. Developing and maintaining the skills and understanding of the game for select basketball requires hours of practice and sacrifices. This means less time for video games and cartoons, going to bed early, eating healthy, studying more, and staying focused on the task at hand. Sometimes, your child

1

may need to skip a school dance to compete in a basketball tournament. Some tournaments take place
on Thanksgiving, Christmas, and Mother's Day. Will
you spend Mother's Day in the gym watching your
son or daughter play basketball?

Your child says they want to play AAU basketball
and is committed to developing their skills. One of
the best indicators of whether your child is serious
about honing their craft is if they practice without
needing your encouragement. I knew my oldest son
was serious at age three because the first thing he
did every morning before breakfast was hunt for his
basketball and shoot hoops in his pajamas. Getting
dressed and eating breakfast were the least of his
concerns until hunger set in, usually an hour or two
later. A second indicator is whether your child is a
student of the game. Do they ask questions about
the game's rules or the distinctions between a post
player, guard, and forward? My youngest son would
sketch plays on my coaching board that he believed
would work in a game. If your child spends time
strategizing, that's when you'll realize they are
developing what most coaches refer to as basketball
IQ. The parents of another young man I coached told
me their son would call out plays in his sleep and
demand the ball. Finally, there's your "gym rat."
Whether your child fits this description is likely

the best gauge of their seriousness about the game. My definition of a basketball gym rat is a child who spends countless hours at the gym practicing dribbling, shooting set shots, jump shots, floaters, layups, and rebounding. A gym rat treats the game like a job that can't even be interrupted for lunch. A gym rat's parents never have to wonder where their child is because the coach or janitor often has to shoo them out of the gym. Coaches may even entrust the gym rat with a key, confident they will lock up when they finish. Not having access to a gym doesn't deter a gym rat from working out, since they will seek out an outdoor court, dribble around the house, shoot paper into a trash can, or practice their form even without a basketball.

If your child decides they do not want to play AAU basketball after a couple of months, I would explore their reasons before allowing them to quit mid-season. Most team sports teach valuable life lessons, and you never want your child to think they can quit when faced with adversity; otherwise, they may struggle to persevere and succeed in anything. We also have the moral responsibility to "Train up a child in the way they should go," which means we must guide and direct them with their best interests at heart. This does not imply we should force them to play by threatening negative consequences if they choose not to. Some common reasons a child may decide they don't want to continue include: lack of playing time, difficulty understanding the game, dislike for physical contact, demanding practices, lack of enjoyment, and, the most prevalent reason, "The coach doesn't like me!" These reasons will be discussed in detail in the following pages. However, if your child says they are not having fun or the game has become too strenuous to enjoy, it may be time for them to take a break until later. This is not necessarily negative. A break can be beneficial on various levels, as long as the child completes the season.

I would never recommend quitting mid-season. They might play football, run track, swim, join the band, participate in debate, engage in politics, or do community work. A child may experience burnout if they start playing too soon and decide against continuing after middle school. Some begin playing late and don't fully grasp the game until their senior year of high school. Nevertheless, our role as parents is to support our children in their pursuits and hope they make wise decisions. Ultimately, the decision to play AAU basketball rests with your child.

FINDING THE RIGHT TEAM

Now that your child has shown a strong interest in playing AAU basketball and is eager to develop their skills and improve, it's time to find them a team. Consider the following five points when searching for the right team for your child.

1. **Cost**
2. **Playing time**
3. **Exposure**
4. **Position**
5. **Organization**

The average cost of participating on an AAU team ranges from $400 to $3000 per child between March and July, depending on your region and the team's level. This price covers food, travel, hotel expenses, tournament fees, and uniforms. The uniforms consist of both a home and away jersey. More elite teams, sponsored by corporate giants like Nike, Reebok, and

Adidas, are required to wear their apparel and include team shoes, shooting shirts, and warm-up gear. The typical cost to enter a team in a tournament is between $200 and $300, not including entry fees for the gym or concessions. The tournament fee contributes to the facility rental where the games take place, pays for game officials, and covers awards like trophies and T-shirts for the winners. Some teams will host their own tournament to help offset AAU costs; some ask parents to pay for their child, but most teams engage in fundraising or seek sponsors.

Some elite teams, such as the Arkansas Wings and the Texas Titans, are fortunate to have sponsors that cover all expenses, including travel, food, hotel, and tournament fees. Kenny Troutt owns the 2010 Kentucky Derby winner Super Saver and the Texas Titans, a basketball organization based in Dallas. I remember watching the Titans play multiple times since my youngest son is just a year behind the original team's graduating class. We never had the opportunity to compete against the Titans, but I still recall being impressed by their character both on and off the court. I understand that most of the kids from the original class, including those from diverse backgrounds, have gone on to receive basketball scholarships and become good citizens. I commend Kenny Troutt because, as a recent Dallas newspaper article noted, he seeks to instill Christian values through daily devotionals and enforce a strict code of conduct for players and parents to provide structure and a sense of purpose.

Playing time is another critical issue parents need to consider when searching for an AAU team. If a child doesn't play, they don't grow, develop, or improve; instead, they become frustrated and bored and may eventually quit the team. One of my most challenging moments as a coach was deciding to step down as head coach and merge with another team. I had valid reasons. At the time, I was coaching my oldest son, who was in the sixth grade. We merged with a team with a major sponsor that could provide team uniforms. We lost a couple of kids that year because we were only given ten uniforms, but watching my son receive limited playing time made that year so challenging. The head coach would take him out when he finally got to play and develop some rhythm. Sometimes, it is beneficial for a child to sit and watch to identify tendencies and strategies, but not for 90 percent of the game. We finished the season strong, making it to the AAU nationals but did not return to that team. Instead, we viewed that experience as one of life's lessons. We moved on to another team the following year.

Most successful AAU teams will have a roster of ten to twelve players at most, with the additional two players aware their playing time will be limited. If a team roster includes more than twelve players, I strongly recommend seeking another team unless your child is one of the standout players. Many AAU teams will organize their rotations like those in the NBA or college level with an eight- or nine-man rotation. The ideal team composition should consist of four guards, four forwards, and two posts.

Just because you volunteer to be the team dad or mom, run the clock during games, keep the stats, or take the lead in fundraisers does not mean your child will get much playing time. This level of basketball focuses on winning and fielding the best possible team to accomplish the task. Paying the required dues or fees does not guarantee that your child will play. I heard one AAU coach state before the season began, "This is not pay to play!" It's essential to understand this. Many kids start playing organized basketball at a young age in a church league, the YMCA, or the Boys and Girls Club. Often, the rules are designed to slow the game, encourage teamwork, and reduce physical contact to prevent injuries. It is cute, fun, entertaining, and equitable—everyone plays equal minutes. Sometimes, depending on the age group, a smaller ball is used, and the goals are lowered to eight feet. Taking the ball from another player is wrong, and the full-court press wasn't a factor. If you go to the games, you get snacks after each game and a trophy or medal at the end of the season for participation. AAU teams don't operate that way.

I spoke with a basketball skills coach who explained that hard work alone is insufficient to earn quality court time. It also requires skills and an understanding of the game. Being 6'5" or 6'8" and very athletic is advantageous, but the point is that your child may need to work on their craft daily to spend more time on the floor.

Exposure is another vital element in your quest for a good team for your child. AAU teams that have existed for over ten to fifteen years and have produced college and professional athletes possess name recognition and attract most college scouts. For instance, the Texas Bluechips is an organization in the Dallas metroplex that is organized, directed, and coached by Mitch Malone. Coach Malone's vision was to establish a structured off-season program for high school athletes in Texas, offering individual instruction, academic tutoring, career counseling, and ACT/SAT preparation. His program has been in place for over twenty years, keeping many kids engaged, active, and off the neighborhood streets, channeling their energy into becoming model citizens and positive role models.

Professional athletes who have come up through the BlueChips organization include Kenyon Martin (New York Knicks) and Chris Bosh (Miami Heat). College athletes include Quincy Acy from Baylor and Damion James from the University of Texas. If you can find a team like the Texas Bluechips, which has had over 1,000 student-athletes receive athletic scholarships since its inception, your son or daughter will gain maximum exposure due to that team's pedigree and history of producing good kids. Attending AAU tournaments and consulting with other AAU coaches nationwide is a great way to find teams comparable to the Texas BlueChips.

However, it is ultimately up to your child to play the game and attract the attention of scouts. Simply wearing a BlueChip uniform does not guarantee success, but it definitely provides a good starting point. This doesn't mean your child should hold off on joining an AAU team until you find one with the most exposure. Most scouts will tell you they don't begin seriously evaluating players until their first year of high school. In the meantime, try to locate an area team that suits your child, allowing them to compete, develop, and better understand the game.

Playing a child out of position is one of the biggest mistakes most parents and some coaches make, and can limit a child's growth and skill development. I required all of my players to handle the basketball and rebound, regardless of their height and weight.

When I graduated from high school in San Antonio, Texas, it was common for guys between 6'3" and 6'7" to play the post position. The teams were strong and dominated their region. However, when they advanced to the state playoffs to face teams from Dallas and Houston, they had to contend with guards standing at 6'3" and 6'5" who were skilled at handling the ball and scoring from the perimeter. They would look over the top of our guards and make entry passes to their 6'9" and sometimes 6'10" post players. We had a lot of heart and desire, but that didn't win games because we faced specific mismatch issues. Losing in the semi-finals or state finals to a Houston or Dallas team is not a tragedy, but what transpired during the recruiting period, when some of our 6'5" post players couldn't handle the basketball or score facing the basket, is. Unless a player is a 6'5" rebounding machine with great instincts, blocking skills, and a forty-inch vertical leap along with heart and desire, you can't help but play the post position once in a while. My two sons weren't the fastest players on my team or their school teams

11

in middle school. They were both a bit chunky, but no one ever questioned their ball-handling skills because I've emphasized the importance of handling the ball since birth. Rebounding requires no specific plays—just the sincere desire to want the ball more than the next guy.

I highly recommend finding a team that allows your child to learn and understand how to play multiple positions without disrupting the team's chemistry. This is important because kids go through growth spurts, and some eventually stop growing. Therefore, the kid who dominated their age group in the sixth and seventh grades is no longer a factor, as they stopped growing and are now playing football. Meanwhile, the kid who could barely play and lacked coordination has grown into their body, stands 6'2", and is scoring in bunches. It is imperative that, at some point during the season—whether at games or practices—you find a team that will teach your child all the positions and nuances of the game.

Finally, organization has always been a pet peeve of mine. Anyone will tell you that I want nothing to do with something that isn't organized. An AAU team that lacks organization is a disaster waiting to happen. Good communication with parents and players, both verbal and written, indicates a great AAU organization, reflecting in the quality of players, coaches, and parents.

The players sit together during tournaments until it's time for them to compete; they eat as a team, and the coaches are easily identifiable by their uniforms. These organizations operate like a well-oiled machine, and problems are swiftly resolved. Consequently, parents can send their kids to out-of-town tournaments without worrying about them.

In today's society, information can be shared through text, email, or apps regarding the next game's location, time, and the opposing team's name. Practice times and locations can be scheduled, allowing players and parents to communicate relatively easily through the same channels. There is no doubt about when the team will leave, where they will stay, and when they will return home.

Understanding where the funds from fundraising, donations, sponsorships, and personal contributions go is essential. This is simply good business practice, and players and parents are likely to support contributing their share to meet financial goals and reduce the stress associated with insufficient funds. Some organized clubs I interviewed do not permit the coach to manage the finances, not because the

13

coach is untrustworthy, but because he is often too occupied with managing and coaching the team. Involving parents and appointing a treasurer, secretary, and team mom is advisable. However, parents must remember that a staff position is not intended to provide more opportunities to advocate for their child.

AAU basketball can be costly, so consider the expense when looking for a team. Anyone interested in playing AAU basketball wants to avoid spending too much time on the bench, so inquire with the coach about the number of players he plans to include on his roster and the team's positional diversity. Competing with a team that lacks a blend of guards, forwards, and post players can be challenging. It would be tough to get sufficient playing time if the team has more than ten players. If your child is in high school and has the skill to play college basketball at any division (NAIA, junior college, or Division I, II, or III), you should consider the possibilities and aim to place them on a team with a strong reputation to boost their chances of being recruited. Lastly, organization is crucial for an AAU team's success. Look at Coach Mitch Malone of the Texas BlueChips, Coach Daryl Richardson of the San Antonio Rohawks, and Kenny Troutt of the Texas Titans. These are just a few teams in Texas that have been established for some time and consistently produce talented players.

DEVELOPING BASKETBALL SKILLS

As noted earlier, being tall, working hard, and maintaining a positive attitude are excellent prerequisites for playing on an AAU basketball team. However, your child must possess basketball skills to stand out from other players and compete. A high basketball IQ combined with a deficiency in the ball skills that make a player a game-changer will result in your child watching many games from the sidelines. Speed and quickness can only take a player so far, especially when genuinely skilled players eventually expose the shortcomings of others. An athletic player who can leap impressively is not ideal at the free-throw line when your team is down by one point and needs to make one free throw to tie the game, followed by a second to secure a win with no time left on the clock. If they shoot an airball and the second shot clips the front of the rim, it's game over!

So your child has told you they will give up video games, TV, and hanging out with friends to focus more on improving their basketball skills. Their AAU team includes some very skilled players, and even though your child is the best player on a club team, YMCA team, and even school team, they are only second in the rotation on their AAU team. What do they lack that the other players have, and how can they develop the skills they need to become better? If your child is no longer the star on the team, there is a reason they are a step or two behind their teammates of the same age and grade level.

AAU basketball teams are comparable to an All-Star team, enabling a coach to field the best players on his roster. Most of those players have worked on their skills outside practice, practicing in the backyard or front driveway to improve. It's possible that as a parent, you did not play basketball and may realize that your knowledge of the game is limited. The coach does not have time to work with your child since he has nine other players to prepare for the weekend tournament. Additionally, the coach might have a family, full-time job, and struggle to teach the game fundamentals because he expects his players to know how to shoot, dribble, and pass. His primary role is to coach, recruit the best talent he can find, and win basketball games.

I have found that several kids on an AAU basketball team participate in basketball camps and/or train with a skills and conditioning coach. Some have bought basketball skill-teaching videos to enhance their abilities.

When my sons were in elementary school, I realized how important it was for them to work on their skills every day. I often shared this insight with my team and arranged a discount if I sent five or more players to a camp. What I appreciate most about basketball camps is the repetition and the instruction, as they allow me to coach and focus on plays. Conversely, what I dislike most about camps is the amount of "dead time," during which the kids are just sitting around. In my view, those camps often lack organization and seem designed primarily to generate profit. They invest heavily in advertisements, and there is no cap on the number of kids who can attend. More often than not, the instructor-to-student ratio is twenty to one, if not worse. As with anything, do your research and find the right camp.

Five Star Basketball Camp has been around since 1966 and has had more graduates playing college or pro ball than any other organization. It was the right choice because each camp guarantees that your child participates in over twenty-five hours of focused instruction and competition. Many of their instructors have experience as high school or college coaches; more than 450 Five Star staff members have coached at the Division I level or higher. Currently, the staff includes NCAA Division I, II, III, and high school coaches who are part of a long tradition of successful coaching in the basketball world. Michael Jordan attended a Five Star Camp and stated, "The camp changed how I felt about basketball and my future. It was the turning point in my life."

Five Star Camp is one of the best camps my sons have attended. I was very impressed with their organization; my sons enjoyed themselves and benefited from the instruction. The atmosphere and intensity at Five Star reminded me of boot camp because they required the campers to stay engaged, disciplined, and maintain a positive attitude, instilling good work ethics. Each day started with a session emphasizing these values. Five Star offers both daytime and overnight camps. They do an excellent job keeping their players focused on a task for an entire week. The camps are held nationwide, and my sons were fortunate to attend Five Star camps.

When training and competing with kids from other states, they experience a different flavor of competition. They discover that kids on the East Coast play differently than those on the West Coast and in the Midwest.

Point Guard College is another camp I endorse, including classroom sessions where players are taught the game. Point Guard College is divided into three different sections: Point Guard College Prep School, Point Guard College Essentials, and Point Guard College. In PGC Prep School, players build a foundation for basketball; in PGC Essentials, players learn to become playmakers at both ends of the floor; in PGC, players learn to think the game and become a floor general. Like Five Star, their camps are intense, with no dead or idle time, helping the kids remain engaged and focused on the task at hand. The instructors do a fantastic job of making the camps enjoyable.

Five Star and Point Guard College are national camps. I encourage you to check them out and invest in your child's learning the skills of the game.

Hiring a personal skills coach is another way for your child to develop game skills, and this approach is popular with high school and college players. For instance, some kids can dribble full speed down the court but haven't mastered techniques like splitting a double team, changing directions without losing speed, or dribbling between their legs or behind their back to create space. Some skills coaches now teach techniques such as the Euro step, floater, and footwork.

Tim Littlefield was the first skill coach my sons met, and they will tell you he was one of the toughest, but also very knowledgeable about the game. Tim was different from other trainers because he didn't charge a fee, yet he trains kids as if he were making $100 an hour. This illustrates his passion and love for the game and his genuine interest in the players' development. He believes that his basketball skills are a God-given gift and that teaching is his way of giving back. His results are just as effective as those of paid skill coaches. This is not to say that you shouldn't pay a personal trainer; if you are pleased with the results, they should be compensated. We offered to pay Coach Littlefield more than once after he trained my sons, yet he refused! So my wife and I gave him a gift card.

Sean Harderman of Ball Hard in Austin, Texas, is another personal trainer my sons enjoyed working with. Sean's workouts are unique because he doesn't emphasize running. He believes that aspect should be handled by the conditioning coach, yet after completing one of his workouts, you feel as though you just ran the 400m dash twice with minimal rest in between. Anyone who has ever run the 400m dash will tell you that your body aches for many days. Sean fosters an environment where players at any level can learn to improve and become more consistent. He also believes that scholarships are essential for success and provides academic monitoring and mentorship.

Finally, there's David Jones, known as "the shot doctor." He is the founder and president of Shooting for Success, a camp that focuses on teaching shooting mechanics. In San Antonio, he is recognized as DJ and works with players of all levels, including Jeremy Lin, a star in the NBA with the Houston Rockets. DJ has experience in professional basketball around the globe, including Germany, India, and Switzerland.

I believe hiring a personal trainer is essential for developing your child's skills at some point in their career. Some kids are quick learners and may not need as much attention as others, but even working with a skills coach during the off-season to hone their abilities will help them improve. It's similar to taking your car in for a tune-up after reaching a certain mileage. Remember, this game has no middle ground—you either work to get better or fall behind.

FINDING THE RIGHT COACH

Finding the right AAU coach can be challenging and isn't always straightforward. The team might be good, but your child may still not enjoy it or feel they are contributing. How often have you heard a child say, "The coach doesn't like me!" Sometimes, parents feel the same way, and coaches and parents frequently end up having lengthy conversations over the phone or at the gym. To avoid such situations or misunderstandings between the coach and player or between the coach and parents, we will explore some characteristics of a great AAU coach.

Most of the AAU coaches I interviewed are volunteers who typically inform the parents and players of this during the first meeting. It's important to remember that they sacrifice their time—family time and sometimes even their vacation time—to coach an AAU tournament. In this chapter, we will focus on some characteristics of a good AAU coach.

23

a) A good AAU coach cares about his players on and off the court.

For instance, when I coached AAU basketball, I asked each player to bring me a copy of their grade slip after each semester because many expressed a desire to play college basketball. My responsibility was to help them understand that they wouldn't have the opportunity to play college basketball if they didn't maintain good grades in elementary, middle, or high school. I aimed to instill good study habits early on, knowing that basketball could be some of my players' only avenue to higher education. While coaching my oldest son's team of fifth graders, a colleague with a successful AAU team shared that several players were struggling academically. He was not interested in engaging with his players' academic progress.

To my knowledge, only one of his players went on to college. I never embarrassed a player regarding their grades but met with them individually before or after practice. I also didn't mind a child missing a practice or two if they had a heavy homework load or an upcoming test because I wanted them to understand the importance of succeeding in the classroom before excelling on the court.

b) A good AAU coach understands the importance of character in AAU basketball.

A player represents his team, community, and family; a good coach must emphasize this. Additionally, a good coach must address character flaws like being disruptive in class, talking back to the instructor, and disobeying parents or societal rules.

I place significant emphasis on my players obeying their parents. Sometimes, a parent asks the coach to counsel the child because the child doesn't respect the parent but seems to respect the coach. Often, parents threaten to remove the child from the team.

I recommend allowing the child to remain on the team but supporting the parents by keeping the child on the bench for the first quarter of a tournament game. I discovered it's much harder for a child to sit and watch their teammates play than to stay home, where they might find other things to entertain themselves. I often found myself in this situation with single moms because the child lacked a father figure at home. I didn't mind counseling as long as I had the parent's permission.

c) Although AAU coaches are not certified dietitians or nutritionists, they care about their players' eating and drinking habits.

I would quiz my players on the four basic food groups and ask if they ate foods in each category because I knew how important it was to their performance on the court. I could observe their food choices when we ate as a team on road trips. My players were prohibited from drinking soda, and we would choose buffets over fast food. I required my players to have one green vegetable and permitted only one dessert. I stressed the importance of eating breakfast before early morning games, explaining that a vehicle without gas won't run.

d) A good AAU coach recognizes how crucial it is to maintain open lines of communication between parents and players.

He is transparent and unhesitant to discuss his decisions and their reasons. He's willing to admit when he makes a mistake and accept his responsibility, whether he erred regarding the gym's location, the start time of a game, the play selection, or the timing of practice. At times, practice will run late because the coach wants to engage with his players before or after the game to discuss strategies. Alternatively, the coach may prefer to communicate solely with the players rather than with the parents. Some gyms offer their locker rooms to their teams, and I made it a point to utilize the facility every chance I got to meet with my players and prepare them mentally before the game.

e) A good AAU coach does not limit a child or hold them back if they are talented and approached by another team that can offer better opportunities. I understand loyalty and team chemistry, but if one of my players could play for the Texas Titans with all expenses covered and a chance to earn a scholarship, I'd support their decision. I could also be selfish and keep the child on my team to enhance my reputation. Consequently, those who do so act out of greed and neglect the child's and parent's best interests. After all, the coach's ultimate aim is to help the child succeed and advance to the next level. It's not about the coach; it's about the player. A good AAU coach strives to place their child in the most supportive environment where they can thrive, grow, and develop into a better player and individual. Sometimes, AAU coaches must set aside their egos and consistently prioritize the child's best interests. And if that situation arises, it's important to remember that everyone can be replaced. Recruit another player and continue coaching.

f) A good AAU coach does not curse at their kids.
I understand that a word or two may slip out during
the heat of the moment, but yelling and shouting pro-
fanities in public at a child or team because of a mistake or a loss is unacceptable. As coaches, we must
never lose sight of our audience, which includes parents, grandparents, aunts, uncles, preachers, school
teachers, and young children. This behavior does not
motivate a player; it only lowers their self-esteem
and undermines their character.

**g) AAU allows many moms and dads to coach
their kids, which is one thing you can look back on
years later and feel proud of.**
I enjoyed coaching both sons, but explained to them
that I would not treat them differently from other players. No favors or special treatments, but I
wouldn't be more demanding on them either because
I didn't want to destroy our father-son relationship
when the season was over. I advised them that they
would have to be among the most demanding working players on the team because their teammates
and parents would view them differently when they
were on the floor. They would expect them to perform well in every game since I would start them
and they would get a lot of playing time. However,
they would spend time on the bench if they weren't
performing well. A good AAU coach recognizes his

child's limitations and helps them improve, but he won't sacrifice winning a game in a critical moment.

If my son is not a good defender, he won't be put on the floor to guard the other team's best player when the score is tied with ten seconds left in a championship game. That's a recipe for disaster. However, I might put him in that situation once he grows and develops, or perhaps during a regular-season game.

h) A good AAU coach won't try to handle all responsibilities alone.
Coaching the team, managing ten different attitudes and personalities every weekend, and practicing at least two or three times a week is a full-time job. Therefore, a good coach recruits volunteers to assist with team transportation and hotel arrangements for players and parents, food, paperwork to meet NCAA requirements, updating AAU information, operating the clock during games, or keeping the scorebook. One coach mentioned that when his team travels, he doesn't allow them to stay in hotels where the doors open to the outside. Another coach stated that his team has a curfew, and he collects cell phones after each player checks in at home. Otherwise, they would stay up all night talking on the phone or playing games. The phones are returned to each player in the morning.

i) Finally, rest is the most important thing a good coach emphasizes repeatedly, especially considering that some AAU teams play every weekend. Most tournaments guarantee a team three to four games; if the team keeps winning, they could play up to three games each day. The combination of a fast food diet and insufficient rest puts kids at risk for injuries and creates a recipe for disaster, leading to a short basketball career. Most AAU teams eat at a fast food chain before, between, and after games because it's quick, affordable, and convenient. While many have improved their healthy food options, most kids still grab a greasy burger from the dollar menu with a soda. Then they return to the hotel, watch TV or play video games, and chat on their phones; soon, it's time for the next game, where they are expected to perform at a high level. There's a reason why these kids often reach the college or professional level with their bodies worn down — they don't get enough rest.

Conducting an informal interview with an AAU coach is perfectly acceptable. I usually write down the questions I want to ask:

1. How long have you coached AAU basketball?
2. How many players are on the team, or how many players do you intend to have on the roster?
3. How often does the team practice, on what days, and at what time?
4. How many tournaments will the team play?
5. Does your son play on the team?
6. What is the cost?
7. Will my son play?
8. Will you help my son get a scholarship?
9. Do you have assistant coaches?
10. Do you have tryouts?

Parents shouldn't hesitate to ask these questions when looking for the best AAU coach for their athletes.

THE PARENT'S ROLE

Attention! Attention! All parents and legal guardians with a child on an AAU team! Please do not coach your child from the stands at any level. In other words, don't coach them from the stands when they are in elementary school, middle school, high school, AAU, church league, YMCA league, or boys and girls club, and don't coach them from the stands when they are playing college or professional ball. By then, they are grown and likely figured out how to play, and if they haven't, it's probably too late, and they won't be in the league for long.

Allowing our children to play on a team means we trust the coach and believe he will make the right decisions for our child and the team. Coaching your child from the stands will only confuse them, as they will be trying to process information from you, the coach, and other spectators who feel qualified to coach from the sidelines. Often, a parent gives instructions that differ from those the coach has drilled into the players all season, which may undo a lot of hard work. I knew a parent fluent in English and German, and when the game began, he would coach his child from the stands and instruct them in German, putting the coach at a disadvantage. Remember that people's voices, opinions, thoughts, accusations, or even well-meaning attempts at help can drown out what the coach is trying to say to help your child make a decision. I've been guilty of this, so I try not to sit too close to the floor or in sight of the coach. The last thing you want is for the coach to see you coaching your child from the stands and not supporting his decisions. This could mean your child won't play because they hurt the team by following your instructions. Parents have excellent intentions, and I know they're trying hard to cheer on their child, but in the heat of the moment, your child needs to hear only the coach's voice. After all, we as parents must trust that the coach will make the best decisions when we put our child on that team. So the best thing to do is sit back, relax, and enjoy the game; when it's over, leave it on the floor and prepare for the next game. Yes, sometimes this is easier said than done, but don't get ejected from the game.

One of the worst things a parent can do is criticize a coach while his wife and family are in the stands. I'm not referring to constructive criticism related to game situations, but gossip has no place in this context. Most coaches voluntarily dedicate their time to coach a team that helps your child grow as a player and person. Some coaches invest countless hours, days, and nights to prepare the team for competition and tournaments. They often work within tight budgets, sometimes even using their money to buy shoes for players wearing the same pair of sneakers for numerous games. Some coaches take in kids over the weekend or during the summer to keep them off the streets and out of trouble while focusing on basketball. I would sometimes have three or four kids stay at my house over the weekend since it was easier than driving back and forth to pick them up when their parents were at work. My wife and I would then prepare breakfast and discuss goals, Christian values, the traits of good citizenship, and respect for others. Often, we discovered that they didn't have these conversations at home. Many coaches do this, and they need our support as parents.

Parents do not receive technical fouls or get ejected from games. Most officials who coach AAU basketball are certified and have been trained in their field. Yes, they will miss some calls, and some more experienced officials will admit when they do. That is not a reason for us as parents to label the official, use profanity, threaten his life, or tell him to "swallow his whistle!" I gained tremendous respect for the men in stripes or gray when I became a certified official and called basketball games for several seasons. Someone from the stands asked me if I had bought my shirt from the Academy Sporting Goods store. It insulted my profession because I took great pride in managing the game and believed I did well. Remember, the official can have a spectator escorted from the venue. When the official is uncomfortable and feels they cannot perform their job, the tournament host is notified. After several warnings, security is alerted, and the fan is escorted out of the gym. I have only been ejected once in my fifteen-year coaching career because my assistant coach continued to harass the official after several warnings. The game was stopped, and we were both asked to leave. When I questioned why I had to go, I was told it was my responsibility to control my bench. So, my assistant and I spent the second half in the parking lot. My son told me one of the parents finished coaching the game, and we lost. So, parents, I say let the coach manage the officials and hope he doesn't get banned from the court.

Coaches are not babysitters, and raising your child is not their job! However, some will step in because they care and want the best for your child. Parents, please pick them up from practice on time. Some of these AAU coaches leave their jobs, fight traffic, coach practices, answer questions from other parents, go home, try to be a dad and husband, and eat dinner late—all because you were an hour late picking up your child from practice and didn't even call. Additionally, never send your child to a tournament without money, expecting the coach to cover emergencies unless the team's fees cover all tournament expenses. Finally, if you don't want the coach to discipline your child, please address discipline issues at home. Nothing is more frustrating than stopping the team van to discipline some players for fighting. Running through the halls and playing on the elevators in a hotel is unacceptable behavior, and it should not be the coach's responsibility to clarify that.

Parents, our role is to discipline our children and ensure they present themselves respectfully in public. Some parents grant the coach permission to discipline their child, though some players seem to respect the coach more than their parents. When I had the authority to discipline one of my players, I helped the child understand their role and the significance of his parents in that process. At times, this was effective, but on other occasions, I had to take more drastic measures to capture their attention, such as reducing playing time. This always grabs every child's attention because they want to play.

Finally, parents, please support the coach's wife because wives are exceptional in that they are the hidden glue that keeps the team together. If they have a child on the team, their role can sometimes be overwhelming, acting as wife, mother, and possibly a mediator between disgruntled parents. A coach's wife often has to listen to the complaints of a parent who is reluctant to voice them to the coach.

Thus, the coach's wife may serve as a buffer or an interpreter, as if English were the coach's second language. One of the biggest challenges of being a coach's wife is having a child on the team and sitting in the stands next to parents who don't support the coach. Therefore, I suggest that the coach's wife sit elsewhere, assist her husband in keeping the books during the game, or help in another way.

FREQUENTLY ASKED QUESTIONS (FAQ)

1. What is AAU basketball?

AAU (Amateur Athletic Union) basketball is a highly competitive program where young athletes can develop their skills, play against top competition, and gain exposure to college scouts. It consists of club teams participating in tournaments across the state, country, and sometimes even internationally.

2. What age groups can play AAU basketball?

AAU basketball is available for kids as young as six and extends through high school. Teams are generally divided into age brackets, often from 9U (under 9 years old) through 17U (under 17 years old).

3. How much does it cost to play AAU basketball?

Costs vary widely based on the team and travel schedule. A typical AAU season can cost anywhere from $400 to $3,000 per child. Expenses may include tournament fees, uniforms, travel, lodging, food, training, and potential private coaching.

4. Is AAU basketball necessary for my child to get a college scholarship?

While AAU can provide valuable exposure to college scouts, it is not the only path to a scholarship. High school basketball, training camps, and personal development are also crucial. However, many college coaches recruit heavily from AAU tournaments because they can watch multiple talented players in one setting.

5. How do I find the right AAU team for my child?

Consider factors such as:
- Cost – What is included in the fees?
- Playing Time – Will your child get meaningful time on the court?
- Exposure – Does the team attend high-profile tournaments
- Coaching – Is the coach experienced and focused on player development
- Organization – Is the team well-run, with clear communication?

6. What should I look for in an AAU coach?

A great AAU coach should:
- Care about player development, not just winning.

- Have experience coaching and a solid reputation.
- Communicate well with players and parents.
- Instill discipline, character, and sportsmanship.
- Focus on skill-building and team chemistry.

7. What if my child doesn't get much playing time?

Playing time is often earned, not given, in AAU basketball. If your child is not playing much, have an honest conversation with the coach about what they need to improve. Additionally, consider whether another team may be a better fit for their development.

8. Does AAU basketball guarantee my child will play in college?

No, but it can increase their chances. Talent, work ethic, grades, and exposure all play roles in whether a player earns a scholarship. Being on a high-profile AAU team can help, but a strong academic record and consistent skill development are equally important.

9. Can my child play multiple sports while in AAU basketball?

It depends on the AAU team. Some teams require a year-round commitment, while others allow flexibility. However, AAU basketball can be very demanding, with frequent travel and multiple games in a weekend, which can make playing another sport difficult.

10. How can I help my child succeed in AAU basketball?

- Encourage skill development outside of practice.
- Support their mental toughness—AAU is competitive.
- Keep academics a priority—grades matter for college scholarships.
- Let the coach coach—avoid coaching from the stands.
- Ensure they get proper rest and nutrition for peak performance.

11. Should I be concerned about AAU basketball burnout?

Yes, playing year-round without breaks can lead to burnout, injuries, and loss of passion for the game. Make sure your child enjoys the process and takes time to rest if needed.

12. What are the biggest benefits of AAU basketball?

- Exposure to top talent and college scouts
- Development of skills and basketball IQ
- Travel and team bonding experiences
- Learning discipline, commitment, and hard work
- Opportunity to build lifelong friendships

13. What should I know about AAU tournaments?

AAU tournaments can be intense, with multiple games in one weekend. Travel is often required, and competition is fierce. It's a great opportunity for development, but it's not for every player.

14. What are common challenges in AAU basketball?

- Unequal playing time – Not all kids will play equally.
- Coach's favoritism – Some teams have politics involved.
- High cost – Fundraising or sponsorships may be necessary.
- Tough competition – The talent level can be overwhelming.
- Parental involvement – Some parents get too emotionally invested.

15. How do I know if AAU basketball is right for my child?

Ask yourself:

- Does my child truly love basketball?
- Are they willing to commit to practices and games?
- Can our family afford the financial and time commitment?
- Is my child mentally tough enough to handle competition and potential setbacks?
- Are we choosing AAU for the right reasons— development and enjoyment rather than just a scholarship dream?

43

16. What should I do if my child wants to quit AAU basketball?

- Find out why—Are they burnt out? Frustrated? Not having fun?
- Encourage them to finish the season—Teaching perseverance is important.
- Explore other options—They may prefer school basketball, recreational leagues, or private training.

17. How can I be a supportive AAU parent?

- Stay positive and let the coach do their job.
- Encourage your child through wins and losses.
- Don't stress about rankings or scouts—focus on improvement.
- Be realistic about your child's skill level.
- Keep basketball fun!

Final Thoughts

AAU basketball can be an amazing experience if approached with the right mindset. It's about growth, hard work, and opportunity—not just scholarships or rankings. As a parent, your role is to support your child's journey and make sure they enjoy playing the game they love.

CONCLUSION

The stage is set, the lights illuminate the floor, and team vans roll into the parking lot, some arriving on chartered buses and others in convoys of cars for the national AAU tournaments. Your child didn't sleep the night before because they were excited and anxious. If they are a junior or senior, they worry about playing well since college scouts will be watching. I've always told my sons to have fun and just play, as you have no control over who sees you and who doesn't. Never let yourself or your concerns get caught up in things beyond your control.

I also reminded them that scouts evaluate you when you enter the gym. Everything counts, from your attire to overall character. They observe how you react to bad calls and coaching instructions, watch your sportsmanship and warm-up routine, and assess your attitude. Players who come in "sagging" (wearing their pants or shorts halfway down their hips) significantly diminish their chances of getting recruited, as showing a lack of respect for others doesn't reflect the qualities of a prime student-athlete.

Upon arriving at the hotel, the teams exit their vehicles dressed in warm-ups—some in khaki shorts and team polo shirts—sporting their game faces and wearing Beats headsets as if they were preparing to compete in the NBA Finals. Yes, it's just that serious, and it should be, considering the amount of time and money invested and the possibility of obtaining a free education. Teams consist of all age groups, from nine and under to high school. The hotel lobby is filled with teams showcasing Nike, Adidas, and Reebok basketball shoes, staring at one another, wondering if they will get a chance to compete while being aware that they are here for a reason, relishing the opportunity to showcase their skills.

As a parent, you are amazed and blown away standing in the land of giants among players you might see on ESPN playing college basketball next year or maybe three or four years later in the NBA. My wife and I watched Shaquille O'Neal play in the AAU national championship game that they won, defeating a team from Indiana. The AAU coach, who met all the qualifications listed in chapter four, had reserved additional rooms in the same hotel to accommodate parents and other supporters of the team. This was

46

always a smart idea as it made meeting with players and parents easy and convenient while fostering a sense of unity between players and parents. The coaches used text messages, emails, and cell phones to inform everyone of game times and locations.

Teams at the national AAU tournament or NCAA national live event tournament typically play one game each day. My wife and one or two other parents would organize the agenda for the team, which included some free educational tours. I know what you might be thinking! You probably say, "Coach Callies, I'm not doing that because the players will be too tired to play." And I agree with you. So we kept an eye on the timing of the tours, and it was very gratifying to see that some of these kids had a chance to experience firsthand things they had read about in the classroom. That is an unforgettable experience. Some of my players had never flown on an airplane until they traveled to an AAU tournament. Indeed, that was a life-changing experience they will never forget. We didn't let the team swim until after the last game of the tournament. I learned the hard way in my early coaching years that swimming works every muscle in your body, especially your legs. Needless to say, we had no energy left in our legs and lost to a team we should have beaten easily because the water drained all our strength.

Now you are seated in a much larger venue than any of the gyms you attended for regular tournaments. The players sit in individual cushioned chairs, and there are three officials instead of two, each with a certified patch, freshly polished shoes, and neat uniforms. A section roped off for college coaches includes some from institutions such as Texas, Alcorn State, Duke, Kentucky, and Union College in Schenectady, New York, all armed with clipboards and programs detailing profiles of each player. These profiles include height, weight, high school grades, and SAT scores. The college coaches are present for one reason: not to cheer for your team's victory. They look to recruit the best player for their pro-gram. Each coach looks for a player with good char-acter, a high basketball IQ, a strong GPA, and SAT or ACT scores. Being ranked is beneficial, but rankings won't secure a spot if you walk into the gym without discipline, show poor social skills, an uncoachable attitude, or skip classes. Good sportsmanship, hard work, basketball skills, supporting teammates from the bench, a positive attitude, and community ser-vice attract college coaches. Prayer always helps too.

The whistle signals the start of the game, impressing parents and players alike, from the nine-and-under division to high school level. When the curtain falls and another champion is crowned, and after you and

48

your child have met and interacted with people from various states, you wonder if it was all worth it and whether you want to continue the journey.

Participating in AAU or select basketball has taken my family and me to places I never thought I'd visit, including Ohio, Kansas, Indiana, Virginia, Nevada, and Florida. Some benefits of playing AAU basketball or any team sport include teaching valuable life lessons like overcoming adversity, allowing players to travel and meet new people, enhancing communication skills, and providing good exposure and great exercise. After completing their basketball career, they can give back to those less fortunate as a coach, official, or sponsor of an AAU team.

**You asked, "Should my child play
AAU basketball?"**

The answer is, "Absolutely!"

ABOUT THE AUTHOR

Arlington Callies was born and raised in San Antonio, Texas, and coached AAU Track for ten years and AAU basketball for approximately fifteen years. He also coaches youth basketball in church leagues and Davis Scott YMCA. In so doing, it allowed him to foster relationships with kids in the community and his church and emphasize the importance of education and being a good citizen. He coached both sons, who played in high school and college. Arlington still enjoys watching the game at all levels and is a loyal fan of the San Antonio Spurs.